WORSHIPPING 24/7

Loveland, Colorado

Group's R.E.A.L. Guarantee® to you:

This Group resource incorporates our R.E.A.L. approach to ministry—one that encourages long-term retention and life transformation. It's ministry that's:

Relational
Because learner-to-learner interaction enhances learning and builds Christian friendships.

Experiential
Because what learners experience through discussion and action sticks with them up to 9 times longer than what they simply hear or read.

Applicable
Because the aim of Christian education is to equip learners to be both hearers and doers of God's Word.

Learner-based
Because learners understand and retain more when the learning process takes into consideration how they learn best.

Worshipping 24/7

Visit our Web site: **www.grouppublishing.com**

Credits
Contributing Authors: Tammy L. Bicket, Mikal Keefer, Julie Meiklejohn, and Mike Nappa
Editors: Tammy L. Bicket and Dawn M. Brandon
Creative Development Editor: Amy Simpson
Acquisitions Editor: Kelli B. Trujillo
Chief Creative Officer: Joani Schultz
Copy Editor: Dena Twinem
Art Director: Jane Parenteau
Cover Art Director/Designer: Jeff Storm
Cover Photographer: Daniel Treat
Print Production Artist: Stephen Beer
Production Manager: Dodie Tipton

ISBN 0-7644-2491-2

10 9 8 7 6 5 4 3 2 1   13 12 11 10 09 08 07 06 05 04

Printed in the United States of America.

CONTENTS

Introduction 4

STUDY 1 **Why Worship?** 7

The Point: *God deserves our worship.*
Scripture Source: *1 Chronicles 16:29*
Psalm 8
Luke 5:1-11
Revelation 5:9-14; 19:5

STUDY 2 **First Things First** 16

The Point: *Your priorities reveal what you worship.*
Scripture Source: *Matthew 4:8-11; 6:19-21, 24;*
10:37-39; 16:26

STUDY 3 **The Power of Praise** 28

The Point: *Praise breaks the chains that bind us.*
Scripture Source: *2 Chronicles 20:1-26*
Acts 16:16-34

STUDY 4 **Entering the Worship Zone** ... 37

The Point: *Real worship is a lifestyle.*
Scripture Source: *Psalms 46:10-11; 150*
Isaiah 58:6-8
Romans 12:1

Changed 4 Life 47

INTRODUCTION

WORSHIPPING 24/7

Quick! What's the first word that pops into your head when you hear the word *worship*? Music? Service? Band? What do you think your teenagers would first think? Would their reaction be positive or negative?

Worship is a word that's heard a lot lately. It's popular to be "into" worship—worship services, worship music, worship bands. But worship is more than a style—it's a relationship—a relationship with our great God. Teenagers need to understand that worship is about growing fellowship and intimacy with a Friend. It's about learning to really know God's character and love for us.

Teenagers need to understand that worship is about growing fellowship and intimacy with a Friend.

The first study will help your teenagers learn that God deserves their worship—but even more, they'll learn why. They'll learn how to spend quality time with God, and they'll ignite the desire to do so. They'll get a chance to discover anew God's power and grace and learn of his desire to have an intimate, personal relationship with each of them.

In the second study, students will learn what their lives are saying about their relationships with God. They'll see that people's priorities reveal what they worship, and they'll be challenged to put God first.

In the third study, your teenagers will discover that there are always good reasons to praise and worship God. Praising God in the midst of hardship and struggle may not seem the natural thing to do, but it's appropriate and brings surprising results. There's power in praise. Praise breaks the chains of our affliction. When we praise and worship God, something always changes—sometimes it's our circumstances, but always, our hearts and attitudes change.

In the fourth study, you'll help students focus on the particulars of real worship—routine-shattering, life-altering, total-involvement, lifestyle worship! Your teenagers will be exposed to the intimacy of worshipping God and will better understand the power, excitement, and joy found in worship as a lifestyle.

Worship can enhance your teenagers' relationships with God and enrich their lives. After completing this powerful series, you and your teenagers may never think about worship in the same way again. Experience worship!

Senior High Bible Study Series

Faith 4 Life™: Senior High Bible Study Series helps teenagers take a Bible-based approach to faith and life issues. Each book in the series contains these important elements:

- ***Life application of Bible truth***
  Faith 4 Life studies help teenagers understand what the Bible says and then apply that truth to their lives.
- ***A relevant topic***
  Each Faith 4 Life book focuses on one main topic, with four studies to give your students a thorough understanding of how the Bible relates to that topic. These topics were chosen by youth leaders as the ones most relevant for senior high students.
- ***One point***
  Each study makes one point, centering on that one theme to make sure students really understand the important truth it conveys. This point is stated upfront and throughout the study.
- ***Simplicity***
  The studies are easy to use. Each contains a "Before the Study" box that outlines any advance preparation required. Each study also contains a "Study at a Glance" chart so you can quickly and easily see what supplies you'll need and what each study will involve.
- ***Action and interaction***
  Each study relies on experiential learning to help students learn what God's Word has to say. Teenagers discuss and debrief their experiences in large groups, small groups, and individual reflection.
- ***Reproducible handouts***
  Faith 4 Life books include reproducible handouts for students. No need for student books!
- ***Tips, tips, and more tips***
  Faith 4 Life studies are full of "FYI" tips for the teacher, providing extra ideas, insights into young people, and hints for making the studies go smoothly.
- ***Flexibility***
  Faith 4 Life studies include optional activities and bonus activities. Use a study as it's written, or use these options to create the study that works best for your group.
- ***Follow-up ideas***
  At the end of each book, you'll find a section called "Changed 4 Life." This section provides ideas for following up with your students to make sure the studies stick with them.

Use Faith 4 Life studies to show your teenagers how the Bible is relevant to their lives. Help them see that God can invade every area of their lives and change them in ways they can only imagine. Encourage your students to go deeper into faith—faith that will sustain them for life! Faith 4 Life, forever!

WHY WORSHIP?

"I am a C. I am a C-H. I am a C-H-R-I-S-T-I-A-N." The teenagers in your youth group may call themselves Christians. They may have heard Bible songs and stories about God since childhood. Others may be just meeting God, being introduced to the Bible for the first time, and learning what it means to be a Christian. But the important question is, Do your students understand what all the stories and teachings have to do with them?

This study will introduce your teenagers to God as a real being who desires a loving, personal relationship with each of them. It will help them begin to understand the important difference between *knowing* God and just knowing *about* him. This study will help teenagers see the awesomeness of a God powerful enough to create the whole universe and intimate enough to be their friend. It will prompt them to respond from the heart with authentic worship.

THE POINT God deserves our worship.

SCRIPTURE SOURCE

1 Chronicles 16:29
Revelation 19:5
Christians are commanded to praise and worship God.

Luke 5:1-11
Revelation 5:9-14
Worship is the natural response when we encounter our awesome God.

Psalm 8
The psalmist expresses wonder at the majesty of God's creation.

THE STUDY AT A GLANCE

#1 For Starters

10-15 minutes

■ **INTRODUCING…GOD!**

What students will do:
Create introductions for God and give thanks for God's presence.

SUPPLIES:
none

#2 Bible Truth

25-30 minutes

■ **AN AWESOME GOD!**

What students will do:
Examine biblical examples of encounters with God that led to spontaneous worship, and discuss attributes of God that have special meaning to them.

SUPPLIES:
- ❑ Bibles
- ❑ newsprint
- ❑ tape
- ❑ marker
- ❑ photocopies of the "Who Is God?" handout (p. 15)
- ❑ pencils

#3 Life Application

10-15 minutes

■ **PRAISE HIS HOLY NAME!**

What students will do:
Create artistic expressions of praise in response to Psalm 8.

SUPPLIES:
- ❑ Bible
- ❑ paint smocks
- ❑ canvases
- ❑ paintbrushes
- ❑ paints
- ❑ bowls of water

■ **BONUS ACTIVITY**
10-15 minutes

Decorate rocks with words and/or symbols of worship and praise.

SUPPLIES:
- ❑ smooth, fist-sized stones
- ❑ acrylic paints, brushes
- ❑ newsprint or dropcloths
- ❑ large plastic bags or smocks
- ❑ bowls of warm water

BEFORE THE STUDY

For "An Awesome God!" activity, make a photocopy of the "Who Is God?" handout (p. 15) for each student. Write the following "worship starters" on separate pieces of newsprint: "God, you are…" "I love you because…" and "Thank you for…" Also, write the following questions on a sheet of newsprint, and tape it to the wall.

• What do you think Simon Peter or the heavenly beings were feeling?

• Why did they respond as they did?

• Why do we sometimes fail to respond to God the way Simon Peter and/or the heavenly beings did?

• Can you think of a time when you felt like Simon Peter or the heavenly beings did? Explain. How did you respond to your feelings?

For the "Praise His Holy Name!" activity, gather canvases or art paper, paints, paintbrushes, and smocks (or large plastic bags with holes for heads and arms). You'll also need bowls of water, and newsprint or dropcloths if you'll be working inside. If you want to do this activity outdoors, check around outside for a suitable place to accommodate all your students. You may wish to play worship music softly in the background as teenagers work on their creations and worship God.

If you decide to do the Bonus Activity, secure a supply of fist-sized, smooth rocks for painting. Provide acrylic paints, brushes, bowls of warm water, newsprint or dropcloths, and smocks or plastic-bag smocks.

FOR STARTERS

10 to 15 minutes

INTRODUCING…GOD!

Have teenagers form pairs, and **say:**

We have a very special guest here with us today—God! In your pairs, decide how you can best introduce our guest to the group. To get started, think of what you would say if you were introducing a good friend. What would you say about that person? Would

you tell about some of the experiences you'd shared? Now apply those ideas to an introduction for God.

Give pairs a few minutes to work, then have them introduce God. When students are finished, **say:**

Thank you very much for your fine introductions! We're going to spend some quality time today with God, discovering anew his power and grace and learning of his desire to have an intimate, personal relationship with each one of us. We're going to learn why God deserves our worship. When we worship God, we spend time acknowledging who he is and how much he means to us. In some ways, it's like encouraging a good friend.

THE POINT

Now I'd like to take a moment for us to thank our guest for being with us today. I'll start in prayer, and then you can share your thanks with God one at a time, silently or aloud. After a few moments, I'll close the prayer. Let's pray.

Begin the prayer by thanking God for his presence with your group and asking him to open your hearts and minds as you discover how to truly know and worship him. Allow a few moments for volunteers to pray, and then close by saying "amen."

This study contains many different forms of worship, including reflection, prayer, Bible reading and discussion, personal sharing, active listening, sensory experience, acts of praise, and affirmation. One important element that is not included is music. If your group would enjoy a musical approach to worship, incorporate a few of their favorite praise songs throughout. Possibilities include "Awesome God" and "I Will Celebrate." These songs can be found in the *Group Songbook*, published by Group Publishing, Inc.

25 to 30 minutes

An Awesome God!

Have pairs join with another pair to form groups of four. Make sure groups have Bibles. Assign half of the groups to read Luke 5:1-11 and the other half to read Revelation 5:9-14. **Say:**

> **Now we're going to hear stories of some who experienced the power of God in a very real way. One of you in each group should read the passage aloud while the rest of the group follows along. After you've read the passage, discuss the questions on the newsprint posted on the wall. You'll be asked to report your answers in a few minutes.**

When groups have discussed the questions, ask volunteers to share their insights. **Say:**

> **Simon Peter was awe-struck when he witnessed the power of God. God's greatness completely overshadowed him. Simon Peter worshipped God because he experienced God. Even the powerful heavenly beings recognized that the power, majesty, and holiness of God completely dwarfed their own. With spiritual eyes, they recognized that God is worthy of all praise and worship. God deserves our worship too.** The Point

Ask two students to read aloud 1 Chronicles 16:29 and Revelation 19:5 while an artistic student draws a simple picture of a throne on a piece of newsprint or on the chalkboard or white board. Tape the "worship starters" that you prepared before class around the throne drawing. **Say:**

> **Not only does God deserve our worship, but God's Word commands us to worship him. So that's what we're going to do right now. We may feel self-conscious at first. We might not even know exactly how to worship him. That's why we have these three "worship starters." Think about how you would complete each of these sentences. When you know what you'd say, come and write at least one response on each sheet. Really think about what God means to you as you write, and we'll be like the heavenly beings, worshipping around the throne.**

Allow students five to ten minutes to complete this activity, then call them back to their groups of four. **Ask:**

- **How easy was it to finish the sentences?**

- Why was it easy or difficult?
- How much does your ability to praise and worship God depend on your knowledge of and experience with him? Explain.

Say: Though we will never fully understand God, what he has revealed to us of himself gives us ample cause to praise and worship him. Learning about the characteristics of God gives us even more reason to worship him.

Give each person a copy of the "Who Is God?" handout (p. 15) and a pencil. **Say:**

Take a few minutes to read through this list of some of God's attributes, and choose one that has special meaning for you. For example, you might choose a characteristic that has been significant in your relationship with God in the past or one that you'd like to know more about. When you've chosen a characteristic, read the Bible verses listed next to it and think about how that attribute can help you know and worship God more fully. If you'd like, you can jot ideas on the back of your sheet.

Allow teenagers about five minutes to work, then **say:**

Share with your group the attribute you chose, and explain why you chose it.

When students have shared, **ask:**

- **After examining some of God's characteristics, why do you think God deserves our worship?** THE POINT

Say: Simon Peter fell to the ground when he saw God's power at work through Jesus. Peter experienced God when he was at work—it had been just an ordinary day for him before meeting Jesus.

Ask:
- **When do you feel closest to God?**
- **How have you seen God in everyday things in your life?**

Say: God deserves our worship, and he wants to be in close personal relationship with us all the time, whether we're working, playing, or even sleeping. God is all-powerful, and he wants to be the center of our lives. THE POINT

LIFE APPLICATION

10 to 15 minutes

PRAISE HIS HOLY NAME!

Set out one canvas and paintbrush for each student. Also set out several colors of paint and bowls of warm water to clean brushes.

Lead students outside, and ask each person to find his or her own spot away from the group (but not too far). **Say:**

We're going to spend some time worshipping God. First, listen carefully as I read one of David's songs of praise to God.

Read Psalm 8 aloud to the group, with feeling and expression. Then **say:**

Now, silently look for evidence of God's creation.

Give students a moment to look around, then **ask:**

- **How do you feel about God's gift of creation? Explain.**

Say: God has given us a truly awesome world to live in, and he definitely deserves our worship. **Now we're going to create special pieces of artwork as an expression of joy and praise to God for the amazing creation he's given to us.** ◀THE POINT

Give each person a smock or large plastic bag to cover his or her clothes, then **say:**

I'm going to read the psalm again, one verse at a time. After I read each verse, express your reaction to what the verse says by choosing one color of paint and painting a few brush strokes on a canvas. You can put the paint on the canvas in any fashion you choose—maybe you'd like to paint a wide, sweeping stroke or a fine, gentle line. Don't worry about making it look perfect. When everyone has painted, I'll move on to the next verse, and you'll move on to the next canvas. Make sure you paint on a different canvas each time, and remember to rinse your brush before changing colors.

Read Psalm 8 again, verse by verse, allowing enough time for teenagers to paint after each verse. After the paintings are finished, have the group step back a bit to admire them. **Say:**

What a wonderful expression of worship you've created.

If your group meets in the city, high schoolers might be distracted by buildings, traffic, and other man-made sights. Encourage students to move beyond the obvious to what their view says about God. For example, teenagers might think about how God gave people the ability to create.

Instead of canvas, you can give each student a piece of card stock, construction paper, or even newsprint. If smocks and paints are unavailable, provide students with markers or crayons in a variety of colors and thicknesses. The point is not the materials you use—it is the artistic expression of worship.

This activity can be done inside with a few adjustments. Lay out newspaper or plastic to protect the floor. To help teenagers experience God's creation, you may want to bring in plants and play a tape of nature in the background. You can also have each person examine his or her hands while thinking about the wonder of God's creation.

Ask: • **How was this time of worship like or unlike other worship experiences?**

• **What's different about worshipping God by yourself compared with worshipping God with others?**

• **Why do you think God's Word says that both are important?**

Have teenagers form pairs, and **say:**

Share with your partner ways that he or she helps you enhance your discovery of the God who deserves our worship. For example, I might say, "Jeff, you help me discover God because you seem to try to find God in everyone."

THE POINT

After pairs have shared, close in prayer, thanking God for being present with the group and for helping teenagers learn how to truly know and worship him.

BONUS ACTIVITY

10 to 15 minutes

If you have time, try this extra activity to complete your Bible study.

Let each teenager select a smooth, sizable rock for this project. Cover worktables with newspaper or dropcloths; have teenagers cover their clothes with smocks. **Say:**

When Jesus rode into Jerusalem on a donkey, cheering crowds surrounded him. They joyfully worshipped and praised him. But the religious leaders were upset that Jesus would accept praise and worship. They wanted him to silence the people's praise. But Jesus responded, "If they keep quiet, the stones will cry out" (Luke 19:40). God deserves our worship. Today we're going to make these stones "cry out" in praise and worship to Jesus.

THE POINT

Give students access to paint, brushes, and water. Instruct them to decorate the rocks with words or symbols of praise and worship directed to God. While they're working, **ask:**

• **What would your rock say to worship God?**

• **Are rocks the only part of nature that praises God? Explain.**

• **How does the glory of God's creation praise him?**

• **Does God's creation ever make you want to praise or worship him? Explain.**

Encourage students to take their praising stones home with them and hold them in their hands each day when they worship God.

***FYI**

You can look outside for rocks that will work for this project. You may even want to take students outside to find their own rocks. Or, if you prefer, you may buy a supply of inexpensive decorative rocks or paving stones from a local home and garden, hardware, or home-improvement store. You might even get a good deal on broken stones. It won't make any difference for this project.

The following chart contains scriptural references and descriptions of God's character.

God is...

All-Knowing	**1 John 3:20**
All-Powerful	Jeremiah 32:17, 27
The Creator	**Isaiah 40:12, 22, 26**
Eternal	Psalm 90:2; 1 Timothy 1:17
Everywhere	**Psalm 139:7-12**
Forgiving	Psalm 86:5; Daniel 9:9; Ephesians 1:7
Good	**Exodus 33:19; 1 Peter 2:2-3**
Holy	Isaiah 6:3; Revelation 4:8
Incomprehensible	**Psalm 145:3; Romans 11:33**
Just	Nehemiah 9:32-33
Merciful	**Exodus 34:6; James 5:11**
One God	Deuteronomy 6:4; 1 Corinthians 8:4
Patient	**Psalm 86:15; 2 Peter 3:15**
The Shepherd	Genesis 49:24; Psalm 23
Truth	**Jeremiah 10:10**
Unequaled	Isaiah 40:13-25
Wise	**Romans 16:27; 1 Corinthians 2:7-11**

STUDY 2

FIRST THINGS FIRST

It's Monday, and an angel secretary takes notes as God dictates. God begins with cosmic issues, then urgent business, then routine stuff. The angel bows to leave, and a scrap of paper flutters out of the Divine Appointment Book and floats to the floor.

God notices. "What's that?" he asks.

The angel shrugs his shoulders. "That teenager called again. I told her you're busy…that you wish you had more time. She said to call when you've got a free minute. She wants to hear from you."

God sighs then wads up the paper and tosses it away. "Well, it's a busy eternal existence. You can't make time for everything."

This is hardly an accurate picture of how God treats your students! But it may be how your students see God. Many teenagers picture God floating somewhere out in orbit—nearby, perhaps, but not seeking their attention. Unfortunately, God may be far, *far* from taking first place in their lives.

But God is a jealous God. He wants first place. He *demands* first place.

With this study you'll help your students recognize where God fits into their lives as they wrestle with making priority choices.

THE POINT Your priorities reveal what you worship.

SCRIPTURE SOURCE

Matthew 4:8-11
We should worship God only.

Matthew 6:19-21, 24; 16:26
Jesus explains the error in worshipping anything other than God.

Matthew 10:37-39
Jesus admonishes us to make God our first priority.

THE STUDY AT A GLANCE

#1 For Starters
10-15 minutes

■ **TIME-WARP ARCHAEOLOGY**

What students will do:
Decide how their rooms reflect their priorities.

SUPPLIES:
- ❑ newsprint
- ❑ marker
- ❑ shovel

#2 Bible Truth
25-30 minutes

■ **GROCERY-BAG SHUFFLE**

What students will do:
Experiment with loading groceries and see how important it is to put first things first.

SUPPLIES:
- ❑ Bibles
- ❑ paper grocery bags
- ❑ assorted groceries
- ❑ loaves of bread and/or cartons of eggs
- ❑ newsprint
- ❑ markers
- ❑ trash can, pot, or bowl
- ❑ "Grocery List of My Priorities" handout (p. 27)
- ❑ pencils

■ **OPTIONAL ACTIVITY**
25-30 minutes

Identify, rank, and discuss their priorities.

SUPPLIES:
- ❑ Bibles
- ❑ stepladder
- ❑ index cards
- ❑ pencils

#3 Life Application
10-15 minutes

■ **JUGGLING PENNY PRAYER**

What students will do:
Explore how they can offer their talents and what they value highly to God to use for ministry and worship.

SUPPLIES:
- ❑ pennies
- ❑ basket

BEFORE THE STUDY

For the "Time-Warp Archaeology" activity, have a shovel, trowel, or whisk broom ready for a prop.

For the "Grocery-Bag Shuffle," obtain one paper grocery bag for each group of three to five students. Be sure to bring extras in case some tear. Gather a large assortment of grocery items of various sizes, weights, shapes, and so on. Divide them up so that each group has at least one large item, one boxed or bagged item, canned goods, and something fragile such as fruit, an empty egg carton, or bread. Bring an extra loaf of bread or carton of eggs for every five to ten students. Provide markers that will write on bread or eggs (you might want to experiment with this in advance—fresh pens with broad tips usually work best on bread). You'll also need a trash can, pot, or bowl. Tape a piece of newsprint to a wall where students will be able to see it. Draw a line down the middle to divide the paper into two columns. Label the first column "Rules for Packing a Grocery Bag." Label the second column "Rules for Prioritizing My Life."

If you choose to do the Optional Activity, consider softly playing in the background a CD of worship music. You may want to bring a six- or eight-foot stepladder to your room to make a visual impression. Have index cards (or small pieces of paper) and a pencil for each student.

For the "Juggling Penny Prayer" activity, you'll need to gather five pennies for each teenager as well as an offering basket.

*NOTES

FOR STARTERS

10 to 15 minutes

TIME-WARP ARCHAEOLOGY

When teenagers arrive, hold up a shovel, trowel, or whisk broom and **say:**

Welcome to the forty-fifth century! You are archaeologists, and you've just uncovered what appear to be homes from the twenty-first century. Your job is to determine what these mysterious people would value most by carefully examining their dwellings. Fortunately, the homes are perfectly preserved. Keep in mind that you know *nothing* about the people who

once lived in these dwellings; you're drawing conclusions only from what you observe.

Ask teenagers to form pairs and **discuss** these questions:

- **In your own dwelling, what appears to be the most important room?**
- **What appears to be the most important piece of furniture?**
- **What appears to be the most precious thing in the dwelling? Explain.**
- **If an archaeologist walked into your room thousands of years from now, what would appear to have been most important to you? Why?**
- **If you could tell a future archaeologist what's most important to you, what would you say?**

Consider adding dramatic flair by decorating your classroom as a classic forty-fifth-century archaeological dig. Wrap the door in aluminum foil; place a "Beware of Falling Skyscrapers" sign on the door; and give teenagers inexpensive, costume-shop pith helmets to wear (or just wear one yourself).

While pairs report what they concluded from their "archaeological studies," list what they say they value most on a piece of newsprint. **Say:**

Our values affect what we worship. Worship is simply adoring something and honoring it. For instance, if you have a car and spend enormous amounts of time and effort paying for it, caring for it, and driving it, you may be worshipping the car. Your priorities reveal what you worship.

Ask:
- **Would anything in your room need to change to show future archaeologists that you worship God? If so, what?**

As a positive counterbalance to their own rooms, you may want to ask students to imagine what Jesus' bedroom would look like if he were a teenager growing up today instead of two thousand years ago. If you have time, you might even want to give small groups boxes, paper, and art supplies, and ask them to create a 3-D model of what "Teen Jesus'" room might look like.

BIBLE TRUTH

25 to 30 minutes

GROCERY-BAG SHUFFLE

Have a volunteer read Matthew 4:8-11 aloud. **Say:**

Satan used all the power and splendor of this world to try to tempt Jesus to divide his love for and worship of God the Father. Even Satan recognized that valuing power, wealth, and comfort more than God is no small matter—it's not much different than serving and worshipping Satan.

Ask:
- **What was Jesus' response to the attractions of this world?**
- **What does his response show us about the possibility of avoiding the temptations to covet or worship the things of this world?**
- **What was the positive result when Jesus chose wisely, making God his priority?**

Divide the class into small groups of approximately three to five students each. Give each group one folded paper grocery bag and a large variety of groceries, enough that it's almost impossible to get them all in. Include items of different sizes, shapes, and types in each group's batch. Give each group at least one large item: a gallon of water, an industrial-size can, a bag of potatoes, or multipack of soft drinks. Be sure each group gets some canned goods, a box or bag of snacks, and something "fragile," like a loaf of bread, fruit, or an egg carton (minus the eggs—just in case). **Say:**

I'm going to give you five minutes to practice packing and unpacking your bag with groceries. Your goal is to get as much in the bag as possible while making sure the bag is stable (so that it won't fall over or rip) and that everything survives intact. Try different approaches, but keep track of what you learn about how and how not to best pack a bag of groceries. When time is up, each group will give a brief demonstration and teach us what you've learned about bagging groceries. Ready? Go!

After groups have learned a thing or two about bagging groceries, call time. Ask each group to unpack its bag and repack it in front of the entire class, explaining why they're doing what they are and what they learned about what needs to go in first. When every

If you prefer, substitute buckets for grocery bags and challenge each team to find the best way to load it with a combination of one very large rock, lots of smaller rocks, pebbles, sand, and jugs of water (to be poured into the buckets as needed or desired). You may wish to evaluate how much is held in each bucket by weighing it on a scale. The point will still be the same: If we don't put the big, heavy item in first, we'll never be able to get it in later. Likewise, God must be our first priority. Worshipping him must come before all other priorities in our lives.

group has had a chance to demonstrate, gather the entire class around the piece of newsprint you prepared before class. **Ask:**

- **What did you learn not to do when packing a bag of groceries?**
- **What did you learn about what had to go in the bag first? Why?**

Say: Let's work together to make a list of rules we could share with others to help them pack a grocery bag correctly the first time.

Write down three to five rules as students call them out. If possible, prioritize the rules so the most important is rule number one (such as, "Put the heaviest, largest items in the bag first"). Then work as a group to come up with appropriate rules for ordering our lives based on each of the grocery rules. **Say:**

Just as the grocery bag can be filled with many items as long as we put first things in first, so we can value and enjoy many good things. Money, clothes, cars, jewelry, and other things aren't evil. God doesn't usually ask us to avoid them altogether (especially clothes!). The problem comes when we value anything—even something good—more than we value God. When this happens, the person, activity, or thing becomes an idol that we worship. Only God deserves our worship. God is the only "treasure" that will last forever.

If your grocery packers had any "accidents"—smashed bread, broken egg cartons, ripped bags—use these as an illustration of the Bible truth. If you have no ready-made examples, make your own now. Then ask a volunteer to read Matthew 6:19-21, 24 aloud, and ask another to read Matthew 16:26. **Ask:**

- **What are some treasures that teenagers may desire or value?**

Give each small group a loaf of bread or carton of eggs. (You may wish to combine groups so you won't need as many loaves or cartons.) Give each group a marker that will adhere to the surface of the bread or egg. **Say:**

Think of all the things that can be very important to people that might be described as treasures of this earth. Write one specific thing on each egg or slice of bread.

Students will find they need to write and handle the items very carefully to avoid breaking the eggs or ripping the bread. When everyone has finished, come together. Let each student read one treasure aloud, then describe how that treasure might be lost or destroyed. For instance, wealth could be lost on a bad investment; a beloved car might be destroyed in an auto accident or taken away by a parent. As students say how each treasure might be destroyed, have them destroy the egg or bread it was written on as a way to illustrate the fragile, temporary nature of anything of this world. You may have students smash or rip up the bread and break the eggs into a trash can, pot, or bowl.

Ask a volunteer to read Matthew 10:37-39 aloud. **Say:**

Jesus talks about some pretty good things here: parents, children—family members we are right to love.

Ask:
- **But what are we not to do—even with truly valuable people, relationships, and things?**
- **What is the consequence of loving anything more than we love God?**

Distribute copies of the "Grocery List of My Priorities" handout (p. 27) and pencils. Encourage students to find a solitary place to work through the handout, examining their own priorities and whether God has first place in their lives.

After they finish the handout, ask students to close their eyes.

Say: Imagine that Jesus is seated in front of you.

Ask:
- **What would Jesus say to you about how you use your free time?**
- **What would Jesus say your priorities are, based on how you spend your pocket money?**
- **What would Jesus say about your energy and focus, based on your conversations with your closest friends?**

Ask students to open their eyes, quietly find a partner, and **discuss** the following questions.

- **Is there a difference between what you say you value most and how you live?**
- **Does anything need to change in your life to make God your first priority? Explain.**
- **How can you begin to make those changes?**

Lead students in prayer. **Pray:**

Jesus, we realize our priorities often reveal that we worship other things in your place. Please give us the courage to make the changes needed to put you first in our lives. Amen.

OPTIONAL ACTIVITY

25 to 30 minutes

Try this activity instead of "Grocery-Bag Shuffle." Ask each pair of students to find another pair and form groups of four. Point to your newsprint list from the "Time-Warp Archaeology" activity. **Ask:**

- **What are other things people value highly?**

Consider playing soft music while teenagers respond to this activity.

As teenagers offer suggestions, add new items to the list until you have fifteen to twenty. **Ask:**

- **Are any of these items fundamentally evil?**
- **Are any wrong to value?**

Cross out any items that your teenagers feel are essentially evil.

Say: The problem comes when we value anything—even something good—more than we value God. When this happens, the person, activity, or thing becomes an idol. Let's take a look at what the Bible says about worshipping anything other than God.

If you have fewer than twelve students, you can simply divide the class as evenly as possible into three groups.

Ask a third of your foursomes to read Matthew 4:8-11; a third to read Matthew 6:19-21, 24; and 16:26; and a third to read Matthew 10:37-39. Direct groups to **discuss** these questions:

- **What do these verses say about worshipping anything besides God?**
- **What are the consequences of worshipping things?**
- **Why do you think God so strongly desires our undivided worship?**
- **How would you sum up these verses in one sentence?**

If your ladder has more than six steps, adjust the number of values you ask teenagers to select. If you don't have a ladder, take your teenagers to a stairway so you can make use of the steps. Or draw a ladder on newsprint and use tape to attach index cards.

Distribute six index cards (or small pieces of paper) and a pencil to each student, and point out the ladder. **Say:**

Now it's time to vote. Pick six of the things people value from our list on the newsprint, and rank them from one to six, with number one being the most important and number six the least important. List one value on each card. When you've finished, place your number-one value on the top of the ladder, the number-two value on the topmost step, and so on until you've placed the number-six value on the bottom step. You have four minutes.

When students have voted, ask volunteers to gather the cards from each step, and total how many number-six, number-five, number-four, number-three, number-two, and number-one votes each value receives.

Say: This is probably what we think our values *should* be...but is it how we're living?

Ask students to spread out a bit and close their eyes. **Say:**

Imagine that Jesus is seated in front of you.

Ask:

- **What would Jesus say to you about how you use your free time?**
- **What would Jesus say your priorities are, based on how you spend your pocket money?**
- **What would Jesus say about your energy and focus, based on your conversations with your closest friends?**

Ask students to open their eyes, quietly find a partner, and **discuss** the following questions.

- **Is there a difference between what you say you value most and how you live?**
- **Are there any idols in your life? If so, how do you feel about that?**
- **Would anything need to change in your life to make God your first priority? Explain.**
- **How can you begin to make those changes?**

Lead students in prayer. **Pray:**

Jesus, we realize our priorities often reveal that we worship other things in your place. Please give us the courage to make the changes needed to put you first in our lives. Amen. THE POINT

LIFE APPLICATION

10 to 15 minutes

JUGGLING PENNY PRAYER

If you have extra time, ask pairs or foursomes to create a pantomime to demonstrate how their values can honor God. While groups take turns presenting their pantomimes, ask viewers to decide what the value is—and how it's being used. Applaud all efforts with enthusiasm.

With their partners from the previous activity, ask students to each identify one of their top personal values and decide how it could be used to honor God. For instance, a talent for basketball could be used to instruct children in the sport and to share faith at the same time.

Ask:
- **Does it change your perspective on worship to realize that what you value can be used to worship God? Explain.**
- **How might your life be different if you began looking for ways to worship God through what you value?**

Ask teenagers to form a circle, and give each teenager five pennies. Ask teenagers not to toss pennies at each other or at anything else.

During this activity, you will ask students to juggle pennies, adding one penny at a time, until they're attempting to juggle five at a time. Be sure to pause while reading directions for teenagers to try juggling an increasing number of pennies.

Ask students to each select their most important penny—the shiniest, oldest, newest, or whatever criteria they choose. **Say:**

> **Because our resources of time, energy, focus, and money are limited, we can juggle just so many things. Juggling one thing isn't all that hard.** Ask teenagers to toss and catch their most important penny. **Juggling two activities is tougher, because they both take concentration.** Try juggling two pennies, and invite teenagers to try also. When they drop their pennies, encourage teenagers to pick them up and try again. Instruct students to juggle more pennies every time you mention a number. **Adding a third,** (pause) **fourth,** (pause) **or fifth** (pause) **makes life all but impossible.**

By this point, pennies will be flying everywhere. Stop the action, and focus teenagers' attention on yourself. **Ask:**

- **Were you able to focus your attention on your most important penny while juggling? Why or why not?**
- **How was this activity like what happens in life?**
- **How do you feel when you're not able to focus on what's important to you?**

Say: **It's hard to give our top value the attention it deserves when we're juggling too many values. It gets lost in the activity or dropped altogether.**

Ask teenagers to collect their pennies and to hold their most important penny in one hand and the other four pennies in the other hand. **Say:**

You lead busy lives. You value many things and many people. Your challenge is to keep your relationship with God the most important thing. Remember, your priorities reveal what you worship.

THE POINT

In a moment, I'll place an offering basket in the center of our circle. If you're willing to make your relationship with God your most important value, it means you've got to give him anything else you value highly. If your job interferes with your relationship with God, you must be willing to surrender it. If a dating relationship interferes with your relationship with God, you've got to be willing to change it. It's up to you to make first things first.

If you're willing to make God first, drop your other pennies in the basket—but hang on to your most important penny. Carry it with you this week as a reminder of your decision. When you drop your pennies in the basket, silently say, "Lord, I give everything to you. You are the most important thing in my life." You don't have to do this—we'll keep our eyes closed until I close in prayer. Only participate if you mean what you're saying.

Ask teenagers to close their eyes and join you for a brief opening prayer. Encourage them to keep their eyes closed and keep praying silently while their classmates step forward and drop their pennies in the basket. (Make sure you participate as well!) Continue in silent prayer as teenagers decide whether to participate. When everyone who wishes to participate has done so, close with a brief prayer.

Grocery List of My Priorities

Make a list of your priorities. Decide what is truly most important to you, and put that first. Put other people, things, and ideals you value in descending order of how important you choose them to be in your life. Then really think about each item. Give an honest estimate of how much time or money you spend thinking about it, doing it, or talking about it.

Next, assess your life. Does your time/money ratio properly match the value each item should hold in your life? Re-rank the items that are the biggest worship risks for you—things that might become more important to you than God if you don't watch it. Mark the item that may be the biggest "worship risk" as number one, the second as number two, and so on.

How much time/money do I spend...

My Priority List	thinking about this?	doing this?	talking about this?	Worship Risk Rank

Am I placing the proper priority on God? Do I worship him with my life?

____

____

What can I do to ensure that I keep God first?

____

____

STUDY 3

THE POWER OF PRAISE

It's easy to praise and worship God when you're on top of the world and everything is going your way. We believe in the goodness and power of God when we see ample evidence of his provision and blessings. But praising God in the darkness of affliction and sorrow goes against everything natural within us.

This study will help teenagers learn that it's just as important—if not more so—to praise and worship God when we don't see clear personal evidence of his power and goodness working on our behalf.

David wrote Psalm 22 during a time of suffering, yet he managed to express his praise to God and his understanding of the power in praising God in the darkness: "Yet you are enthroned as the Holy One; you are the praise of Israel" (Psalm 22:3). Another translation states that God inhabits the praise of his people.

Today, your teenagers will study two Bible stories in which God's people, under great duress, responded to their difficult circumstances with victorious shouts and songs of praise. God responded by defeating their enemies, breaking their chains, and freeing them from impossible circumstances. God still inhabits the praise of his people. When your students learn to praise and worship God in the midst of storms and troubles, they'll find that God still changes things. He may not always make the problem go away, but he always changes our fear, discouragement, frustration, and sorrow into peace, joy, and faith in his goodness and power.

THE POINT **Praise breaks the chains that bind us.**

SCRIPTURE SOURCE

2 Chronicles 20:1-26

God delivered Israel when the people praised him.

Acts 16:16-34

Paul and Silas sang praises in prison, and their chains were broken.

THE STUDY AT A GLANCE

#1 For Starters

10-15 minutes

■ APPLAUSE, APPLAUSE!

What students will do:

Clap and cheer, depending on how they feel about particular scenarios.

SUPPLIES:
none

■ BONUS ACTIVITY

5-10 minutes

Discover the key for being freed from the rubber bands that bind them.

SUPPLIES:
- ❑ rubber bands
- ❑ scissors

#2 Bible Truth

25-30 minutes

■ PRAISE REPORTS

What students will do:

Form two television news teams and report "live" from the scene of today's Bible passages with an emphasis on the power of praise to change things in bad situations.

SUPPLIES:
- ❑ Bibles
- ❑ microphone props
- ❑ "WPTV News Reports" handout (p. 36)

#3 Life Application

10-15 minutes

■ BREAKING THE CHAINS

What students will do:

Create paper chains, each link representing a difficulty or problem they may be facing, and break the chains as they praise God.

SUPPLIES:
- ❑ assorted colored construction paper
- ❑ scissors
- ❑ markers
- ❑ tape

BEFORE THE STUDY

For the "Praise Reports" activity, make several copies of the "WPTV News Reports" handout (p. 36), and cut them in half for the two news teams. If you want to allow students to actually record and play back their news reports, make arrangements to have a video camera and someone who knows how to use it for each team. Also provide a TV to show the reports afterward.

For the "Breaking the Chains" activity, cut yellow, blue, red, and orange pieces of construction paper into strips to make paper chains. Make strips one to two inches wide across the entire short length of a piece of construction paper. Be sure to make at least two strips for each student.

FOR STARTERS

10 to 15 minutes

APPLAUSE, APPLAUSE!

Say: I'm going to describe some circumstances that a teenager might encounter in the course of his or her life. We're going to measure how you feel about each circumstance by how loudly you applaud. If it makes you feel very good or happy, applaud loudly. If you're not quite as excited about it, clap less enthusiastically. If you don't feel like applauding at all, that's OK too. Are you ready to make your feelings known?

Read these entries one at a time, allowing time for applause to recognizably build or die down before reading the next one.

- **You get an A on a difficult, important test after asking God to help you.**
- **You gave your last few dollars to the church offering, and the next day receive fifty dollars in the mail.**
- **School tomorrow is unexpectedly cancelled.**
- **The person who has been making your life miserable at school moves away.**
- **Your parents inform you that they'll buy you the new car of your dreams for your next birthday.**
- **Your cranky old neighbor turns out to be a billionaire—and when she dies, you discover she has left it all to you.**

- **Your house is destroyed by a tornado.**
- **You're paralyzed in a car accident.**
- **You're beaten and thrown in prison, though you've done nothing wrong.**
- **Your country is invaded by a more powerful nation.**

Feel free to add scenarios that you know will either delight or appall your group. Next, **ask:**

- **Why did you applaud so strongly for some items, but not for others?**
- **Why was it easier to embrace some events more than others?**
- **How would you feel about God if some of the good events happened in your life? Why?**
- **How would you feel about God if one of the bad things happened to you? Why?**
- **Is God somehow less good or less powerful when bad things happen in our lives? Explain.**
- **If God deserves our praise and worship when things are going well for us, does he deserve our praise and worship less when we go through difficulties? Explain.**
- **How have you responded to God during difficult times in the past?**
- **How would you want to respond to God during times of trouble?**
- **How easy would it be for you to praise and worship God during difficult times?**

Say: It's not always easy to praise and worship God when we feel frightened, mistreated, sad, or in pain. But God still deserves our praise. And something wonderful happens when we praise God in our darkest days. The power of God is unleashed in our hearts and in our circumstances. Praise breaks the chains that bind us. THE POINT

Let's examine some wonderful examples of this in the Bible.

BONUS ACTIVITY

5 to 10 minutes

If you have time, try this extra activity idea after "Applause, Applause!" Give each student a rubber band. Show them how to use it to each bind a hand in the following manner:

1. Hook one end of the rubber band around the thumb.
2. Stretch the rubber band across the back of the hand.
3. Hook the other end around the little finger.

Say: Without touching anything at all—including your hand or any other part of your body—try to get free from the rubber band. When you get it off, stand up. If you decide you can't get it off by yourself, kneel and raise your hand.

It's unlikely that teenagers will be able to remove the rubber bands using only the affected hands. When students come to this conclusion, kneel, and raise their hands, go to them quickly and snip the band with scissors. When students have finished, **ask:**

- **What were you thinking and feeling as you tried to free yourself from the rubber band?**
- **Did it get easier or harder as you worked at it?**
- **Why was it so difficult for some of you to stop struggling against the rubber band on your own?**
- **How is the rubber band like difficult circumstances that happen in people's lives?**
- **What are some things people do to struggle against hardships?**

Say: When problems and difficult circumstances afflict us, the natural human response is to struggle against them on our own to try to fix them. It's easy to focus on the problem and to grow frustrated. But it's important that we turn to God when life gets too difficult. God has the power to deliver us. It's easy to praise and worship God when he does deliver us, but even when he doesn't, he still deserves our praise and worship. Praise breaks the chains that bind us. Praising God always changes things. Sometimes it changes our circumstances. Sometimes it just changes us, bringing us closer to God, where we can rest in the peace of his presence.

THE POINT

*FYI

If some students actually do succeed in removing the rubber band, it won't ruin the illustration. Simply **say:**

God gives us the wisdom and ability to take care of many difficult situations ourselves. But there are some problems that are just too big for any of us.

BIBLE TRUTH

25 to 30 minutes

PRAISE REPORTS

Divide the class into two groups. Assign one group 2 Chronicles 20:1-26; assign the other group Acts 16:16-34. Give each group several copies of the half of the "WPTV News Reports" handout (p. 36) that pertains to their Bible story. **Say:**

> **Your group is a news team for WPTV (Worship and Praise TV). You've been assigned a story for today's news broadcast. Your job is to get out there, interview the people involved, and put together a story that will give viewers insight on the power of praise in the midst of difficult circumstances.**
>
> **Look at your sheet and the possible people on your list to be interviewed. Everyone in your group must be involved and must either ask or answer a question (or questions) "on the air." Decide how many interviewers you will use and who will play what parts based on the number of people in your group. Take seven minutes to read through your Bible passage and prepare and practice your interviews. At the end of that time, you'll get a chance to present your interview to the rest of the class. Remember, your focus in presenting your story is to show the power of praise.**

If your group is large, you can have more than one person doing interviews and being interviewed, or have several teenagers be part of a group of people (such as the people who gave Jehoshaphat bad news) so that everyone can participate. If your group is small, you could have just one teenager represent a group of characters, have students take on multiple roles, or simply reduce the number of characters.

After seven minutes of planning and rehearsal, allow the groups to take turns presenting their interviews. Then **ask:**

- **If you were in Jehoshaphat's or in Paul and Silas' place, how difficult would it be to praise the Lord?**
- **Why do you think these people worshipped and praised God in spite of their bleak circumstances?**
- **How do you think these experiences influenced their attitudes the next time they faced trouble?**
- **How should it affect your attitude when you face difficult situations?**
- **How might an attitude of worship affect you or your difficult situation?**

If possible, provide video cameras, and allow groups to record their interviews and play them for the rest of the class like a real news report.

Say: Jehoshaphat, Paul, and Silas learned the power of praising God even in the darkest of days. We can learn from their experiences that praise breaks the chains that bind us and delivers us to a place of sweet release and fellowship with God.

LIFE APPLICATION

10 to 15 minutes

BREAKING THE CHAINS

Divide the class into four groups. Give each group a stack of colored construction paper strips all in the same color. Give each group a different color of paper strips. **Say:**

Every person has problems or goes through times of difficulty. These problems or circumstances are like chains that bind us in fear, discouragement, disappointment, frustration, and suffering. Today we're going to make paper chains to represent these spiritual and physical "chains" that sometimes threaten to bring us down. In your group, brainstorm as many difficulties as you can think of in the category that you're assigned.

Make assignments according to the following chart:

Group	Paper Color	Category	Examples
1	Yellow	Fear	Sickness, dying, failing
2	Blue	Discouragement/ disappointment	Feeling inadequate, being betrayed
3	Orange	Adversity/ problems	Injustice, being poor
4	Red	Suffering	Being sick, being rejected

Have groups write difficulties in their category—at least two per student—on the strips of paper with black markers. On the back of each strip, they should write one thing they could praise the Lord about in that situation or in spite of it.

After five minutes, instruct groups to divide the strips evenly among their members, then call the groups back together. Use the strips to make a paper chain of difficulties. Start by having a member of the first group read aloud the difficulty on the first strip, then the praise on the back, before taping the strip into a loop. A person from the next group should do the same, linking his or her strip through the first loop. Continue with this process, alternating colors and students, until a complete chain has been made.

When the chain has been completed, gather together in the center of the room. Weave the chain through the students, wrapping within it as many teenagers as is practical. **Say:**

This chain represents a lot of problems. It also represents a lot of reasons to praise God. Praising God breaks the chains that bind us. I'd like everyone to think of one difficulty or problem you're facing right now. Close your eyes, and say a silent prayer, asking God to help you and give you the courage to trust and praise him in spite of that circumstance.

THE POINT

Allow a moment of silent prayer. Then pray out loud, asking God to lift the chains of difficulty from teenagers' lives, but more important, to give them an overcoming attitude of praise and worship.

Then **say:**

Let's praise God right now. Say your praise out loud, just as Jehoshaphat's people did and like Paul and Silas did. Say whatever comes into your head or heart. Let's shout to the Lord, "Praise the Lord!" Let's say, "Thank you, Lord. Your love endures forever."

As teenagers worship and praise God out loud, encourage them to pull against the paper chains and break them as an illustration of God's power to change them and their circumstances when they praise him.

WPTV News Reports

2 Chronicles 20:1-26: Israel Threatened by Powerful Enemies

Possible Participants in Your News Story

News anchor

Reporter/Interviewer

King Jehoshaphat

People who gave the bad news to Jehoshaphat

People of Judah

Jahaziel

People who sang praises to God

A warrior who didn't have to fight

Possible Interview Questions

- What role did you play in this situation?
- How did you feel about the situation?
- What were you thinking when Jehoshaphat prayed?
- Were you scared?
- What made you able to praise God?
- What did God do when you praised him?
- How do you feel about the Lord and the situation now?

TIPS

- Be sure you tell the basic story through your interviews or commentary.
- Add your own questions to bring your story to life.
- Keep your focus on the importance of praising God in difficult circumstances.

WPTV News Reports

Acts 16:16-34: Paul and Silas in Jail

Possible Participants in Your News Story

News anchor

Reporter/Interviewer

Paul

Silas

Jailer

Other prisoners

A person near the jail

Possible Interview Questions

- What role did you play in this situation?
- How did you feel about the situation?
- What were you thinking when Paul and Silas prayed?
- What did you think when the earthquake struck?
- Were you scared?
- What made you able to praise God?
- What did God do when you praised him?
- What did you learn about God's power and the importance of praising him?
- How do you feel about the Lord and the situation now?

TIPS

- Be sure you tell the basic story through your interviews or commentary.
- Add your own questions to bring your story to life.
- Keep your focus on the importance of praising God in difficult circumstances.

ENTERING THE WORSHIP ZONE

Unfortunately, in many teenagers' minds these days, worship has been stuffed neatly into a box that's far too small. To such people, worship is limited to that slice of a church service when the latest Scripture songs are sung. For others, worship is a style of music that differentiates some Christian artists from others who sing pop, rap, or gospel.

But worship is so much more than a style of music or part of a church service. Worship is a lifestyle. What's more, worship is a lifestyle God calls all Christians to practice daily.

Today's study is a perfect opportunity to revolutionize your teenagers' concept of worship—and revolutionize their lives as well. This study will help teenagers recognize three distinct and active parts of worship: praise and adoration of God, reverence and respect for God, and service to God.

Armed with today's knowledge and a little practice, your students will be ready to plug worship into every aspect of their daily lives. They can adopt the worship lifestyle. What a way to live!

THE POINT

Real worship is a lifestyle.

SCRIPTURE SOURCE

Psalm 46:10-11
The psalmist tells us to be still and know God.

Psalm 150
The psalmist urges us to praise God in many ways.

Isaiah 58:6-8; Romans 12:1
The writers encourage us to worship God through serving others.

THE STUDY AT A GLANCE

#1 For Starters
10-15 minutes

■ WORSHIPPING THE MESSIAH

What students will do:
Tell the story of how George Handel wrote the "Hallelujah Chorus" and listen to the song.

SUPPLIES:
- ❑ "Hallelujah Chorus" handout (p. 46)
- ❑ recording of Handel's "Hallelujah Chorus"
- ❑ audiocassette or CD player

#2 Bible Truth
20-25 minutes

■ MINI-MARATHON OF PRAISE

What students will do:
Examine Psalm 150, then spend time praising and adoring God in various ways and silently revering him as they meditate on Psalm 46:10-11.

SUPPLIES:
- ❑ Bibles
- ❑ paper
- ❑ pencils

#3 Life Application
15-20 minutes

■ SERVICE WORSHIP

What students will do:
Worship God by serving others then discuss Isaiah 58:6-8 and Romans 12:1.

SUPPLIES:
- ❑ Bibles
- ❑ supplies needed for service project (see p. 43)

■ OPTIONAL ACTIVITY
15-20 minutes

What students will do:
Write a psalm, prayer, song, or poem of personal worship to God.

SUPPLIES:
- ❑ paper
- ❑ pens

■ BONUS ACTIVITY
up to 5 minutes

What students will do:
Spend time singing praise to God.

SUPPLIES:
- ❑ praise and worship songbook

BEFORE THE STUDY

For the "Worshipping the Messiah" activity, make a copy of the "Hallelujah Chorus" handout (p. 46), and cut apart the sections. Locate a copy of Handel's "Hallelujah Chorus" to play for teenagers, and bring a CD player or some other means of playing the music in class.

For "Service Worship," determine which service project or projects you'd like teenagers to participate in (see p. 43 for ideas), and collect the needed supplies.

FOR STARTERS

10 to 15 minutes

WORSHIPPING THE MESSIAH

One excellent contemporary recording of the "Hallelujah Chorus" can be found on the CD *Handel's Young Messiah*. Published by Word Records, it should be available at your local Christian bookstore.

After everyone has arrived, form four groups (a group can be one person). Give one volunteer in each group a different section of the "Hallelujah Chorus" handout (p. 46). **Say:**

Let's start off today by learning the story of one of history's most well-known worship songs, the "Hallelujah Chorus." In your groups, listen as someone reads your section of the story, and be prepared to retell that section of the story to someone else. Ready? Go.

Give groups a few minutes to listen to and learn their sections of the story. When teenagers are ready, have them find partners from each of the other groups to form new groups of four. Be sure each foursome has all parts of the story represented. Then, starting with the person who learned Part 1 of the story, have teenagers take turns telling their sections of the story to their partners.

While teenagers are telling each other the story of how Handel wrote the "Hallelujah Chorus," set up an audiocassette or CD player to play a recording of that song.

When everyone has heard the complete story, **say:**

Now I'd like us to take a few minutes to listen to the worship song Handel said gave him a glimpse of God. As you listen, think about how the song makes you feel about God.

Play the "Hallelujah Chorus" (if possible, turn it up loud). Have foursomes **discuss** these questions:

- What feelings about God did you have as you listened to the "Hallelujah Chorus"?
- Why do you think worshipping God through this song made Handel feel like he was in God's presence?

Say: Worship is a powerful and intimate expression of our relationship with God. We need to know, however, that worship is not simply something that happens at church or on a special occasion. Real worship is a lifestyle and involves three things: praise and adoration of God, reverence and respect for God, and service to God. Let's explore what that means.

THE POINT

BIBLE TRUTH

20 to 25 minutes

MINI-MARATHON OF PRAISE

Have teenagers stay in their foursomes from the previous activity. Distribute paper, pencils, and Bibles to each group.

Say:

In your foursomes, read Psalm 150. (Pause while teenagers read the Scripture.) **In your groups, write five to ten answers to this question:**

- **What does Psalm 150 tell me about worshipping God through praise and adoration?**

After three minutes, have someone from each group report the results of his or her group's discussion. **Say:**

Now, instead of just talking about worshipping God through praise and adoration, we're going to *do* it!

Spend several minutes leading teenagers in a mini-marathon of praise. You may want to choose three to five of the praise activities that follow, or use some of your own. Here are some ideas you might try:

- Sing a familiar praise song.
- Give God a one-minute standing ovation.
- Form a circle, and have everyone tell one thing he or she likes about God.
- Have foursomes create imaginary "God Awards" (such as "Best Father of All Time" or "Most Likely to Love"). Then have foursomes "present" their awards to God.
- Lead teenagers in shouting out the words of Psalm 150.
- Have teenagers each tell a partner about one time they knew God was active in their lives.
- Have teenagers imitate musical instruments for one minute to create a "praise orchestra" for God.
- Starting with the letter A and ending with the letter Z, have teenagers think of words to describe God that begin with each letter of the alphabet.

After the mini-marathon of praise, gather students in a circle. Have teenagers volunteer their responses to these questions:

- **What went through your mind during our mini-marathon of praise?**
- **How do you think God felt about our mini-marathon of praise?**
- **Why do you think Psalm 150 tells us to praise God?**

- **What makes it easy or difficult for you to praise God each day?**
- **How might spending time in regular praise and adoration of God affect your daily life?**

Say: Real worship is a lifestyle, and that includes learning how to praise and adore God on a regular basis. Worship also involves an attitude of reverence and respect for God. Let's take a few moments right now to experience what that can be like.

Have teenagers each find a private spot in the room, free from distractions, where they can either sit or kneel. Make sure each person has a Bible open to Psalm 46:10-11.

When everyone is in place, **say:**

We're going to spend the next three minutes in complete silence. As we experience the silence, read Psalm 46:10-11 several times, and ask God to help you follow the instruction of the Scripture.

For some teenagers, two minutes of silence may seem like an eternity. For others, three minutes may be only enough time to get them started. You know your group best, so feel free to adjust the time to fit your group's personality.

Encourage teenagers not to be distracted by others during this time of silent reverence. Time three minutes of silence.

After three minutes, have teenagers find partners to **discuss** these questions:

- **Describe the feelings you had while we were silent.**
- **What did you discover about worship as you silently read Psalm 46:10-11 and then acted on what you read?**
- **Why do you think it's unusual for us to worship God by simply sitting quietly before him?**
- **What are other ways to show reverence and respect for God?**

Ask pairs to share any insights gained from their discussions. Then **say:**

Real worship is a lifestyle. Each day we're given the opportunity to worship God through an attitude of reverence for God and respect for others. While we're still in an attitude of quiet reverence, let's take a moment to pray for each other.

Encourage partners to spend the next minute or so praying for each other, either silently or aloud. Ask teenagers to pray that their partners experience the peace that comes from reverently and respectfully worshipping God during the coming week.

LIFE APPLICATION

15 to 20 minutes

SERVICE WORSHIP

Say: Real worship is a lifestyle. So far we've learned that worship includes praise to God and reverence for God. A lifestyle of worship also includes service for God and others. In just a few moments, we're going to leave our classroom and worship God by serving others in our church. But before we go, brainstorm with your partner ways you can serve someone and return to our room within five minutes.

THE POINT

Have pairs brainstorm ideas. If teenagers seem stuck, suggest ideas such as the following:

- Take out the trash.
- Clean a bathroom.
- Sing a song for an adult class (make sure ahead of time that this is OK with the adults).
- Wash car windows in the church parking lot.
- Pick up trash in the sanctuary (if no one is meeting there).
- Pick up trash around the church grounds.
- Clean out drinking fountains.
- Create a newsprint thank-you card for the pastoral staff, and hang it in the church lobby.
- Write appreciation letters to members of the youth staff.
- Wash chalkboards in empty classrooms.

When teenagers are ready, have everyone synchronize their watches, then send them out in pairs to perform at least one act of service. Remind teenagers to be back in five minutes.

After teenagers return, have pairs join together to form foursomes. Have groups read aloud Isaiah 58:6-8 and Romans 12:1. Have groups **discuss** these questions:

- **What did your pair do to serve someone?**
- **How was that, in some small way, a fulfillment of what Isaiah 58:6-8 and Romans 12:1 tell us to do?**
- **Why do you suppose God considers service a form of worship?**
- **When is it difficult for you to serve others? Explain.**
- **What's one thing you can do this week to worship God by serving others?**

After the discussion, have foursomes rejoin the large group,

If your group is unable to leave the classroom, have teenagers look for ways to serve within the room. For example, they could straighten up the classroom, set up chairs for the next class, draw an encouraging mural on the chalkboard, leave a "Well Done!" note for the custodian, and so on.

If your group meets in a home, have teenagers look for ways to serve each other or the hosts during this activity. For example, teenagers might straighten the meeting room, wash any dishes used for refreshments, or trade shoulder rubs. Allow teenagers to go outside if weather permits. They can pull weeds, sweep the walk, or water flowers and trees.

and allow time for teenagers to share any interesting insights they gained. Then **say:**

> **Encouraging others is also a way of serving. So right now, let's take a moment to encourage each other.**

In turn, have teenagers complete this sentence with two encouraging words that describe the person on their left: "[Person's name], God has blessed you with [blank] and [blank] that you can use to worship him." For example, a teenager might say, "Tony, God has blessed you with a great laugh and a helpful attitude that you can use to worship him."

End this study with a brief prayer, asking God to make each of your students a "walking worship zone" during the coming week.

*NOTES

OPTIONAL ACTIVITY

15 to 20 minutes

If you'd like, try this Optional Activity instead of "Service Worship."

Distribute paper and pens to students. Encourage them to write a personal prayer, psalm, song, or poem of worship to God. It should express their feelings to God. **Say:**

> **Take a few minutes to express your worship to God by writing a prayer, song, psalm, or poem. The form and style of what you write isn't as important as writing what you're feeling about God. Write as though you were talking directly to him. Tell him what you love and appreciate about him. Tell him how you desire to worship him with your lifestyle. Tell him what he means to you. If you don't know how to get started, think about one or all of the three aspects of worship: praise and adoration, reverence and respect, and service. Sharing what you write will be optional.**

THE POINT

Allow students seven to ten minutes to find a comfortable spot where they can get alone with God and to put their worship into words. Allow time for students who want to share their worship writing to do so. Of course, worship can be very personal and private, so don't coax or pressure anyone to read or perform what he or she has written.

BONUS ACTIVITY

up to 5 minutes

If you have time, try this extra activity to conclude your Bible study.

Gather everyone in a circle. **Say:**

> **Worship is a powerful force in our lives, and real worship is a lifestyle. Today we've experienced worship through music, praise, silent meditation, and service. The more you begin to incorporate these and other forms of worship into your daily lives, the more worship will become your lifestyle.**

THE POINT

Ask teenagers to share one thing they learned during this study and one way they plan to worship God through their lives this week. Give teenagers a moment to think before asking for their responses. When teenagers have shared, **say:**

> **Before we go today, let's experience once more what it feels like to be one of God's "worship zones."**

Lead teenagers in singing several praise and worship songs. Use songs familiar to your teenagers that also focus on giving praise and adoration to God. If you have more than five minutes of meeting time left, allow students to continue worshipping until the end of the meeting.

If your group isn't musical, lead students through some of the ideas that you didn't use earlier from the mini-marathon of praise.

Any of the following praise and worship songs would be an appropriate closing. All can be found in the *Group Songbook*, published by Group Publishing, Inc. They are: "As the Deer," "Awesome God," "Father, I Adore You," "Great Is the Lord," "How Majestic Is Your Name," "I Will Celebrate," "I'm Gonna Sing, Sing, Sing," "King Jesus Is All," "Sing Hallelujah to the Lord," and "Victory Chant (Hail, Jesus, You're My King)."

Photocopy and cut apart this handout for use during the "Worshipping the Messiah" activity.

Part 1

More than 250 years ago, George Handel was a musical composer living in England. He accepted an assignment to write the music for a new collection titled *Messiah.* A unique aspect of this collection was that all the words were taken directly from Bible passages.

Part 2

As he began writing the music for *Messiah,* composer George Handel became consumed with his task. He was so caught up in the worshipful activity of creating this masterpiece that he often simply forgot to eat or sleep.

Part 3

One of the most memorable parts of George Handel's musical was titled "Hallelujah Chorus." Using the words of Scripture, this song is approximately five minutes of powerful and triumphant praise to Jesus. This song has become Handel's most remembered work.

Part 4

Just after George Handel finished writing the "Hallelujah Chorus," his servant came into the room. He found Handel sitting at a table, with tears streaming down his face. "I did think I did see all heaven before me," said Handel, "and the great God himself."

(Adapted from *George Frideric Handel: His Personality and His Times* by Newman Flower)

CHANGED 4 LIFE

To help students take what they've learned into their daily lives after they've finished this study, distribute small notebooks or journals to everyone. Challenge each student to keep a daily worship journal. The goal is to think about worship, spend time worshipping, and write at least something every day for an agreed-upon time (two weeks or a month). So that it doesn't feel overwhelming, assure teenagers that they don't have to write much. They can write a few sentences describing their worship experience, or they can write words of praise and worship instead.

Remind teenagers that worship can include many different aspects: praise and adoration, respect and reverence, and service to God. Caution them not to get stuck in a worship rut, but to worship God in a variety of ways.

At the end of the set time, get together for a time of reporting and joint worship. You may wish to schedule such an event outdoors under the stars, where it's easy to truly recognize and embrace God's vast greatness. The darkness can also make it easier for teenagers to share their personal insights and feelings about what they've experienced and how they've grown over the past weeks. Encourage teenagers to continue their daily worship journals. Don't forget to allow time for corporate worship before concluding your meeting.

Look for the Whole Family of Faith 4 Life™ Bible Studies!

Senior High Books

- *Applying God's Word*
- *Believing in Jesus*
- *Christian Character*
- *Family Matters*
- *Following Jesus*
- *Is There Life After High School?*
- *Prayer*
- *Sexuality*
- *Sharing Your Faith*
- *Worshipping 24/7*
- *Your Christian ID*
- *Your Relationships*

Junior High Books

- *Becoming a Christian*
- *Choosing Wisely*
- *Fighting Temptation*
- *Finding Your Identity*
- *Friends*
- *God's Purpose for Me*
- *How to Pray*
- *My Family Life*
- *My Life as a Christian*
- *Sharing Jesus*
- *Understanding the Bible*
- *Who Is God?*

Preteen Books

- *Being Responsible*
- *Building Friendships*
- *Getting Along With Others*
- *God in My Life*
- *Going Through Tough Times*
- *Handling Conflict*
- *How to Make Great Choices*
- *Peer Pressure*
- *Succeeding in School*
- *The Bible and Me*
- *What's a Christian?*
- *Why God Made Me*

The Youth Bible

The Bible to use with Faith 4 Life.

Visit your local Christian bookstore,
or contact Group Publishing, Inc., at 800-447-1070.
www.grouppublishing.com